What on Earth? Tornadoes

What on Earth?

What's this?

Turn the page to find out.

Published in 2005 in the United States by Children's Press,
an imprint of Scholastic Library Publishing,
90 Sherman Turnpike, Danbury, CT 06816

ISBN 0-516-25321-2 (Lib. Bdg)

A CIP catalogue record for this title is
available now from the Library of Congress.

Printed and bound in China.

Editors: Ronald Coleman
Sophie Izod
Senior Art Editor: Carolyn Franklin
DTP Designer: Mark Williams

Picture Credits Julian Baker & Janet Baker
(J B Illustrations): 6-7, 8(t), 9(t) 10-11, Nick Hewetson: 9(b),
15(t), Corbis: 8, 13, 25, 28, 29, 31, Digital Vision: 16, 26,
TOPEX/Poseidon Team/CNES/NASA: 18,
John Shaw/NHPA: 18 Dr. Joseph Golden/NOAA: 3, 23,
National Weather Service Forecast Office Albany NY: 12,
NOAA Photo Library/NOAA Central
Library/OAR/ERL/NSSL: 1, 14, 17, National Weather
Service Forecast Office Knoxville TN: 15, NOAA/ Historic
NWS Collection: 22, Topfoto.co.uk: 21

Cover © Jim Zuckerman/Corbis Images

What on Earth?

Bang!
It's a giant hailstone.
Tornadoes often happen at
the same time as
thunderstorms, heavy rain
and huge hailstones.

**Crack! Bang!
Flash!**

What on Earth? Tornadoes

DAVID AND HELEN ORME

What do we call a tornado over the sea?

Turn to page 22 to find out!

children's press®

A Division of Scholastic Inc.

NEW YORK • TORONTO • LONDON • AUCKLAND • SYDNEY

MEXICO CITY • NEW DELHI • HONG KONG

DANBURY, CONNECTICUT

Contents

What on Earth?

Raining frogs?

Sometimes, a tornado scoops up frogs or fish and carries them into the sky. They may surprise people by coming down in the rain far away.

Cro-o-a-a-k!!!!

Introduction

A tornado is wind that spins around very fast, forming a funnel shape. It moves along destroying everything in its path. Tornadoes are extremely dangerous, mostly because they pick up pieces of buildings, trees, bits of metal and even cars. The biggest danger from a tornado is getting hit by some of this debris.

Where are the most tornadoes?

Three out of four of all the world's tornadoes happen in the United States. There is an area in the middle of the United States where tornadoes are so common that people call it Tornado Alley.

How fast can a tornado go?

Tornadoes are the fastest winds on the planet. The fastest tornadoes spin at about 250 miles (402 kilometers) per hour. Most tornadoes spin more slowly than this.

What Happens When a Tornado Hits?

As the tornado spins, it moves along the ground, sucking air into the bottom and forcing it upwards. Powerful tornadoes are like giant vacuum cleaners, sucking up objects such as cars or even buildings, causing major destruction. A tornado is not the same thing as a hurricane. Tornado winds are much faster but they don't usually travel as far or cause as much damage as a hurricane.

How big are they?

Most tornadoes are small. A typical tornado makes a path 50 yards (46 meters) wide and 1 to 2 miles (1.6 to 3.2 kilometers) long. The largest tornado path can be 1 mile (1.6 kilometers) wide and the smallest less than 10 yards (9 meters) wide. The damage path can be 50 miles (80 kilometers) long!

Anvil-shaped thundercloud

Hailstones

Rain

Funnel (vortex)

What on Earth?

Flat-top?

Thunderclouds have a flat top. Some people say that a thundercloud looks like a blacksmith's anvil.

Where Do Tornadoes Occur?

Tornadoes can happen anywhere, but they are most common and most severe in the United States, India and Bangladesh, a small country next to India.

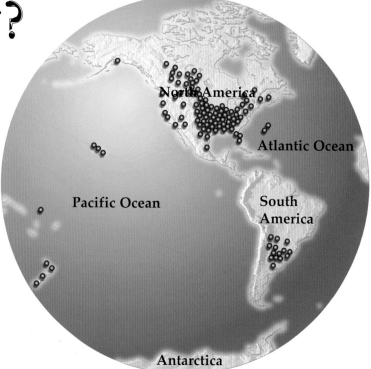

Areas around the world where tornadoes occur are shown on these two maps (*above*)

What time of day?

Tornadoes are most common in the late afternoon. All day, the sun has warmed the ground. As the air above begins to cool, hot air rises from the ground to meet it. When the warm air meets the cold air, a tornado may form.

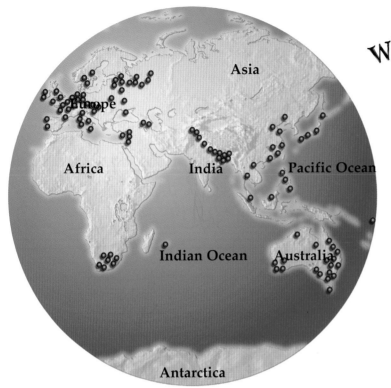

Asia

Europe

Africa

India

Pacific Ocean

Indian Ocean

Australia

Antarctica

What time of year?

Tornadoes can strike thoughout the year, but in some places spring and early summer are the main seasons they occur. This is because there are changing wind patterns in spring and summer.

What is a twister?

Tornadoes (*right*) are also known as twisters or whirlwinds. They are smaller than cyclones. The dark funnel-shaped column of a tornado moves along the ground at 20 to 70 miles (32 to 113 kilometers) per hour.

How Are Tornadoes Formed?

Tornadoes usually begin with thunderstorms. Some thunderstorms blow wind down to the ground. Sometimes, though, warm air swirls around and up into the cloud, and a funnel-shaped column of the thundercloud reaches toward the ground. If the column of cloud then touches the ground a tornado is born.

Winds at the upper level push the tornado along

Where do tornadoes get their energy?

Tornadoes get their energy from the thunderstorms they come from. Only a tiny amount of the energy in a thunderstorm is used in the tornado. This tells you how powerful thunderstorms can be!

What on Earth?

Why do tornadoes spin?

When two fast winds move in different directions and at different speeds, the air between them spins. To see why, put a pencil between your hands. Move one hand towards you and one away from you. The pencil will spin!

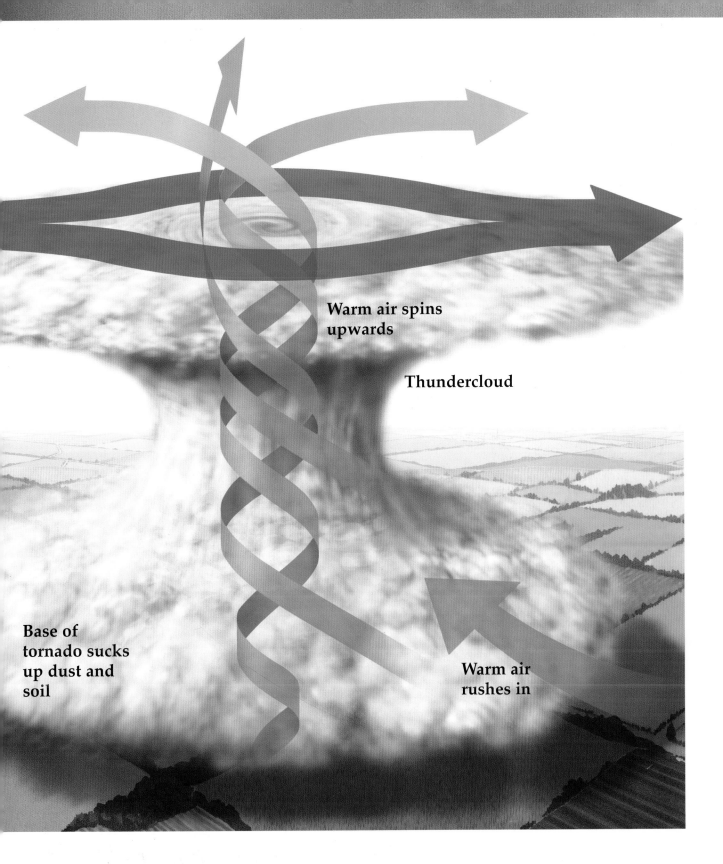

Warm air spins upwards

Thundercloud

Base of tornado sucks up dust and soil

Warm air rushes in

How Do We Measure Tornadoes?

Scientists use special equipment to figure out the diameter of a tornado's funnel, how fast it travels, and how fast it spins. The most important measurement is how fast it is spinning, because the faster it spins, the more dangerous it is. Scientists estimate a tornado's speed by the amount of damage it does.

Who was Professor Fujita?

Professor Theodore Fujita (1920-1998) invented the "Fujita Scale" to estimate the speed a tornado spins. Category F0 with winds less than 73 miles (117 kilometers) per hour causes light damage.

F1, at 73-112 miles (117-180 kilometers) per hour, can push a car off the road. F5, at over 260 miles (420 kilometers) per hour, can lift a house from its foundation.

Can tornadoes skip?

No they can't! Many people think that when a tornado doesn't touch the ground for a while it is "skipping". Wrong! A tornado that is not touching the ground is just a storm!

How Are People Warned?

It is impossible to forecast where a tornado might strike until it's very close. When forecasters think there is a risk, they give warnings on radio and television. In some areas, there are tornado sirens. When people hear these they should take shelter. However, because there are many false alarms, people may ignore warnings.

How does radar help predict tornadoes?

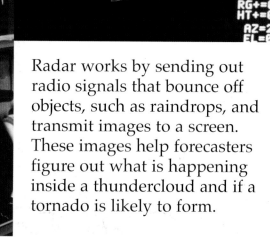

Radar works by sending out radio signals that bounce off objects, such as raindrops, and transmit images to a screen. These images help forecasters figure out what is happening inside a thundercloud and if a tornado is likely to form.

How do forecasters get information?

Weather forecasters analyze information from weather stations and then tell us what sort of weather we can expect.

What on Earth?
Who gets warnings?

The U.S. weather service is very experienced in predicting tornadoes, but in countries where tornadoes are rare, or where there isn't a good weather service, little or no warning is possible.

Forecasters get information about weather conditions from satellites, weather stations, weather balloons, airplanes, and radar. Even with all the modern technology available, it is hard to tell exactly when and where a tornado will hit.

Watch out! Tornado on the way!

Who Are Storm Chasers?

Storm chasers are people who like to get as close as they can to storms and tornadoes. They may be scientists who study weather, or just people who enjoy the excitement of being close to one of nature's most amazing events. Some storm chasers earn a living by selling close-up photographs and videos of tornadoes.

What are they waiting for?

These chasers are waiting to photograph a tornado. They may have traveled hundreds of miles to see it.

What sort of equipment is used?

Many storm chasers use fast, safe vehicles, equipped with scientific instruments to measure wind speed, air pressure and humidity. They may even have portable radar.

How dangerous is it?

Very! The wind is dangerous, and so are heavy rain, hailstones and objects that tornadoes throw into the air.

What on Earth?

How big can a hailstone be?

The storms that create tornadoes can produce hailstones that weigh almost 2 pounds (1 kilogram), which is the size of a grapefruit!

Bang! Crash! Ow!

Where Is Tornado Alley?

Tornado Alley is a large part of the United States where a lot of tornadoes occur. It stretches from Texas in the south to North Dakota in the north, and east of the Rocky Mountains. There have been tornadoes in most American states.

Where are the Rocky Mountains?

The Rocky Mountains stretch from southwest United States to northwest Canada.

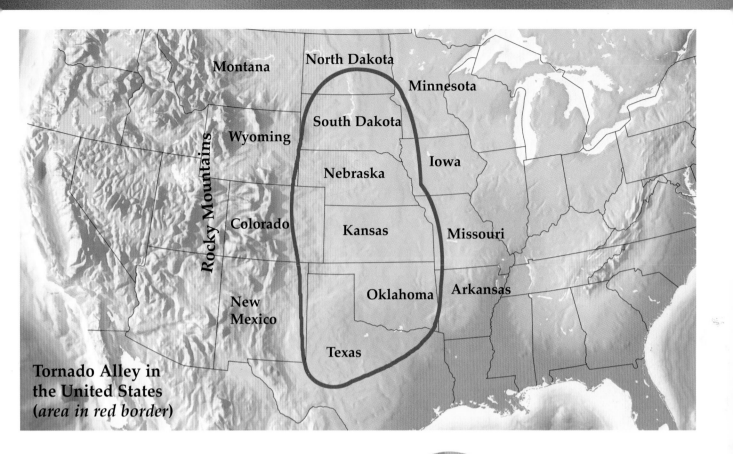

Tornado Alley in
the United States
(*area in red border*)

Why do tornadoes happen in Tornado Alley?

Weather systems over the Rocky Mountains
pull in cold winds from Canada in the
north. Warm winds from the southeast are
full of water vapor from the ocean. These
winds are pushed upwards when they reach
the mountains, where they meet the cold air.
These are perfect conditions for tornadoes
to form.

Underground?

Many people who live in the
states that are part of
Tornado Alley have special
places to go when a tornado
is coming. Some have
underground spaces where
the family waits as the
tornado passes over them.
Watch "The Wizard of Oz"
which takes place in Kansas!

Where Was the World's Worst Tornado?

Bangladesh is a poor country. People must live where their crops grow, even if the area is in danger of floods and storms. They cannot escape easily because the roads are rough making travel difficult. Their homes are not sturdy enough to withstand strong storms. If crops are destroyed there may be nothing else to eat. The world's deadliest tornado struck Bangladesh in April, 1989. Over 1,300 people died and 50,000 lost their homes.

What on Earth?

How long does a tornado last?

A tornado can last from several seconds to over an hour!

The photograph (*right*) shows the effect of a cyclone on Bangladesh in 1991. A lot of people were able to use special storm shelters that had been built since the last major disaster. However, more than one-and-a-half million homes were destroyed, and many people lost their lives.

Sandwip Island off the coast of Bangladesh, four days after the cyclone hit

Can Tornadoes Happen at Sea?

Tornadoes at sea are called "waterspouts". Actually, they are columns of water vapor, not water. Like tornadoes, they are usually formed by thunderstorms, when warm air meets cold air. This may happen when cold air crosses a warm current in the sea. Waterspouts can happen anywhere, but are especially common in the seas around Florida in the United States.

How dangerous are waterspouts?

Waterspouts have less energy than land tornadoes. They do not pick up and throw objects but they can be powerful enough to damage or sink large boats. They aren't reported in tornado records unless they hit land.

What's the Bermuda Triangle?

It is an area of the Atlantic Ocean. Stories tell us that many ships have mysteriously disappeared there. Perhaps waterspouts are to blame.

Are Tornadoes Getting Worse?

Many scientists believe that the world's weather is getting warmer. If the sea is warmer, the winds coming from it will have more energy. When this energy is released in thunderstorms, the tornadoes will become stronger.

What's the evidence?

In the 1950s, around 500 tornadoes were recorded each year in the United States. By the 1990s, the average was over 1,000 a year.

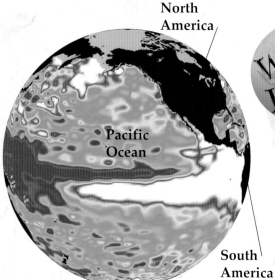

North America

Pacific Ocean

South America

The satellite picture (*above*) shows *El Niño*. The two white areas are large masses of warm water flowing towards North and South America.

What on Earth?

What is "El Niño"?

Every few years, there is an unusual current of warm water called *El Niño* in the Pacific Ocean. *El Niño* does not directly cause tornadoes, and it is hard to say if it has had anything to do with the number or force of recent tornadoes.

How strong is the evidence?

In the 1950s, scientists may not have known about tornadoes in remote areas. There may just seem to be more now, because more are being detected. Tornadoes do more damage now than in the past, but this may be because more land is covered by houses and factories.

What's the Best Kind of House to Live In?

The best kind of house to live in is one built to survive tornadoes. Builders and architects are trying to create tornado-proof buildings. People in older homes can build "safe rooms" inside their houses, reinforce their basements, or build underground shelters. The worst kind of house to live in is a mobile home.

This house (*below*), was struck by a tornado. Its roof was blown away and its walls were blown down.

What on Earth?

What was the worst tornado in Tornado Alley?

The worst tornado to strike Tornado Alley was the Tri-State tornado of March 18, 1925. It left a 219 mile (342 kilometer) trail of destruction across three states, killing 695 people.

How Would You Survive A Tornado?

If you go to a place where tornadoes are common, it is important to learn about how to stay safe. Everyone should know in advance what to do when a tornado hits. Don't wait until one is about to strike! Pay attention to weather forecasts so you can be warned and can head for safety.

What to do checklist

Learn to watch the sky. Look out for very **dark storm clouds**. Hail may be a sign a tornado is on its way, and so is **garbage falling from the sky**. Learn to listen for tornadoes. You may hear a **rushing sound**, which soon becomes a roar. Look out for leaves being pulled upwards by the wind. Most of all, **watch out** for **funnel-shaped clouds!**

Tornado dangers

Outside The worst place to be when a tornado hits. Find shelter as quick as possible.

Flying debris Kills the most amount of people during a tornado. Stay away from windows, doors and anything that is not bolted down.

Vehicles People often think they are safe in their cars or trucks, but tornadoes can pick vehicles up killing the people inside. If you can, leave your car or truck and find a sturdy building.

Keep a supply of candles and batteries for a flashlight in case the power goes out. Listen for warning sirens and move to a shelter immediately. If you can, wear a helmet, this may save your life if the roof caves in. If you can't move to a shelter, sit under a table and cover yourself with cushions and pillows to protect yourself from flying debris.

Tornado Facts

No one is sure where the word "tornado" comes from. Some people think it is from two Spanish words, "tronada," an old word for thunderstorm, and "tornar," meaning to turn.

A tornado that hit Oklahoma city in May 1999 may have been an "F6" with winds around 320 miles (510 kilometers) per hour. We can't be sure though, since there is no way to measure tornadoes more destructive than an F5.

You can go on a storm-chasing vacation. There are companies that promise to get visitors as close as possible to a tornado, then get them safely away again. It's more exciting than lying on a beach!

The sky sometimes turns a greenish color before a tornado hits.

In 1915 in Kansas, five horses and the rail they were tied to were carried ¼ mile (0.4 kilometers) by a tornado. They were found unhurt, still tied to the rail.

The longest recorded distance a tornado has traveled is 293 miles (477 kilometers) in 1917.

Glossary

Bermuda Triangle an area in the Atlantic Ocean where ships and aircraft have disappeared

condense to turn from a gas to a liquid when cooled

cumulonimbus clouds towering clouds with a flat base, seen in thunderstorms

current water or air moving in a particular direction

diameter the distance across something circular, like the funnel of a tornado

estimate use facts to make a guess

Fujita Scale a scale invented by Professor Theodore Fujita to estimate the spin speed of a tornado by seeing how much damage it has caused

humidity the amount of water vapor in the air

hurricane a powerful tropical storm

radar a way of detecting objects at a distance by making radio waves bounce off them

storm cell the rotating clouds in a thunderstorm

vortex a spinning column of air

water vapor water in the form of a gas

weather balloon a balloon with equipment to measure weather conditions high in the atmosphere

What Do You Know About Tornadoes?

1. What is the difference between a tornado and a hurricane?

2. How fast does an F5 tornado spin?

3. Which country gets the most tornadoes?

4. Where is Tornado Alley?

5. How are people warned about possible tornadoes?

6. How do people protect themselves from tornadoes?

7. What should someone do if they are in a car when a tornado is coming?

8. What are tornadoes over the sea called?

9. Are there more tornadoes now than in the past?

10. What is the most dangerous thing about tornadoes?

Tornadoes are very common in Oklahoma. Can you guess how often one is likely to hit any single area there?

Index

Pictures are shown in **bold.**

Answers

1. A hurricane is a violent tropical storm affecting a wide area. A tornado is faster, but affects a much smaller area (See page 6)
2. Over 260 miles (420 kilometers) an hour (See page 12)
3. The United States (See page 5)
4. In the United States, stretching from Texas to North Dakota (See page 18)
5. By radio and television, and in some places, warning sirens (See page 14)
6. By building storm shelters, safe rooms or basements in their houses (See page 26)
7. Leave the car and find shelter in a strong building (See page 27)
8. Waterspouts (See page 22)
9. We don't know. More are being recorded, but there may not actually be more happening (See page 25)
10. Objects being blown around (See page 5)

Even in Oklahoma, a single area is only likely to be hit in exactly the same place once every 700 years!